DEDICATION

For my city cowgirl, Edie,
who dreams of farm country and many mouths to feed.

To our good friend, Bella, who loves animals so much! ♡

Hazel grazed in her pasture and dreamed.

She dreamed of a time when her hooves struck soft dirt and sent a plume of it behind her as she raced down a track lined with cheering faces.

Her tail flicked away the thought like an annoying biting fly.

"Oh Hazel, you silly old nag," she said to herself. "There's no shiny gold cup waiting for you now so you best stop dwelling on it."

She went back to her grazing and gave up the dreaming.

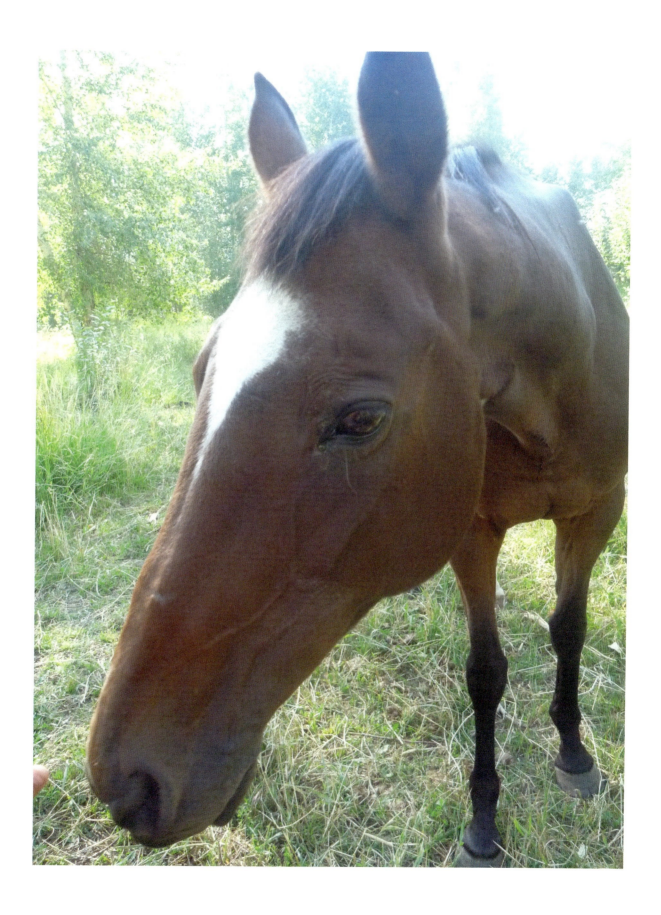

A reluctant city girl named Edie had her own fair share of dreams. She yearned for the gentle sway of long grasses and the nudge of a soft muzzle accepting a carrot from her palm.

"Oh Edie, you silly girl," she said to herself. "There's no point wishing to be somewhere you can't. Better put all this foolishness out of your head and get back to work."

Edie pulled out her homework packet and sharpened her pencil.

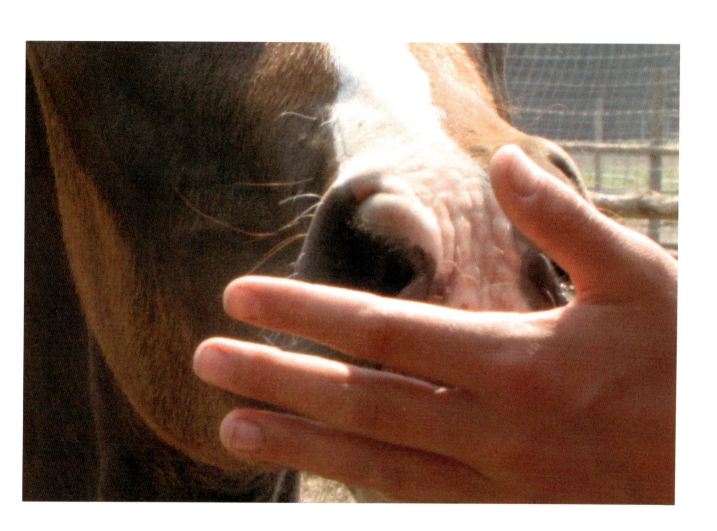

The days lingered on and Hazel continued her grazing and Edie her pencil sharpening until . . .

SUMMER!

Now, nothing changed at first.
Hazel fought off dreams of carrying a proud rider on her back and Edie shoved away thoughts of blacks and bays, dapples and grays.

Then, one fair June morning
Hazel curiously sniffed the air.
The scent of adventure was undeniable.
It came in from the West and smelled of
cedar trees, roses and rain.

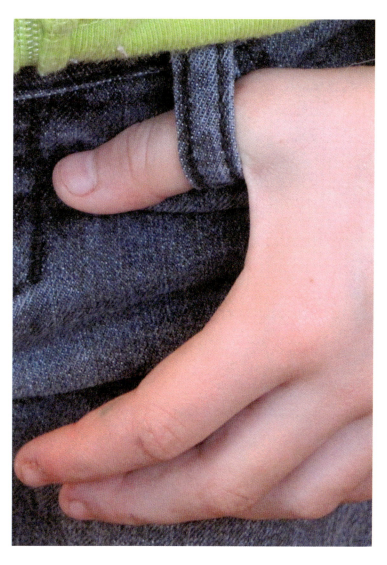

Edie also felt the twinge
of adventure.
It shot up her spine like
a bolt of lightning
striking a Douglas Fir.
She wanted to hop
right out of her summer
sandals into
a pair of cowgirl boots
and her thumbs ached
to hang from the belt
loops of a sturdy pair of
jeans.

Mama & Papa Portland couldn't fail to notice that their little girl had a longing to fill her lungs with clean country air.

Words tumbled out of their mouths before they could catch them, "Edie, how would you like to spend a summer with Grandma and Grandpa Idaho?"

Edie's feet broke into a gallop around the kitchen because those feet had a strong feeling Grandma & Grandpa Idaho knew where to find pastures and horses.

Cowboy Tony knew what Hazel dreamed about. He also knew that what she really wanted, even more than a gold cup, was to feel important again.

"There's nothing better for an old horse than a young girl," he mumbled as he rummaged through his truck bed looking for carrots.

"Now where on God's great earth did I put those carrots?" he wondered, scratching his head under his dusty hat.

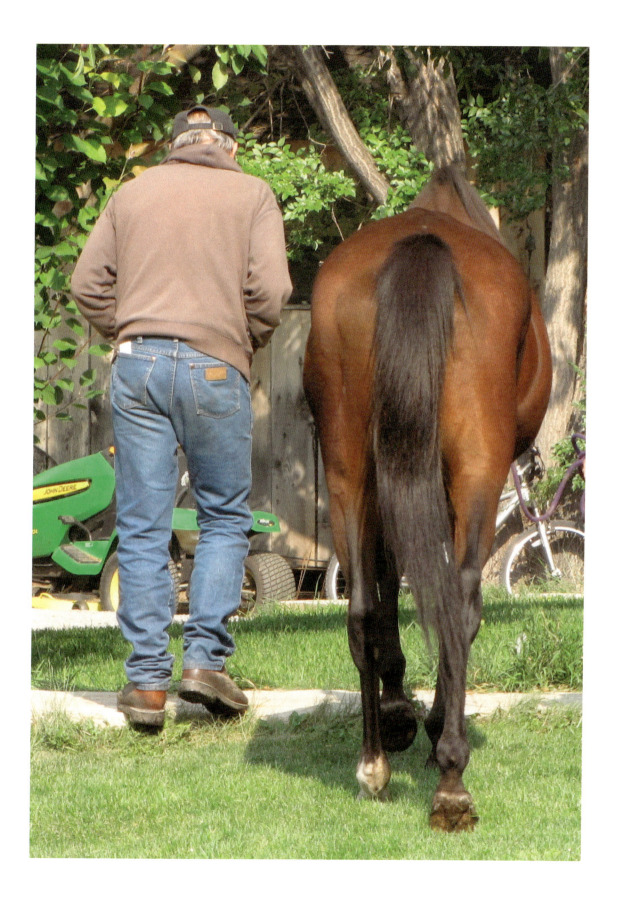

A whole week went by at Grandma & Grandpa Idaho's place and despite wearing her best cowgirl attire Edie hadn't met up with a single horse willing to have her as a rider.

She offered the Arabians at the fancy ranch crunchy apples and they only snickered at her. She reached out her hand to touch their soft noses and they snapped at her with their white teeth.

"We are way too important for a tiny human like you," they said. "We were bred for princes and kings. We race across deserts drinking the wind. Go and talk to the pony."

Grandma & Grandpa Idaho took Edie to the fairgrounds hoping she'd find encouragement from the rodeo queens. They looked so confident sitting on top of their steeds. But, those horses had no patience for a young girl.

They wanted to prance and rope and flash their hooves to the crowd.

They thought that the only real horse was a spirited one, not an old ninny who'd allow a baby to climb up on her back.

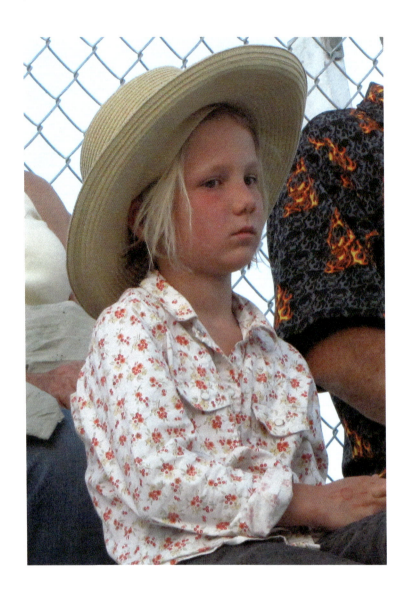

With every whoop and holler from the crowd, Edie's heart sank deeper into her boots. She was beginning to believe she'd never meet a horse willing to make her into a real cowgirl.

Grandpa Idaho looked at Grandma Idaho
and whispered, "You know as well as I do that
there's nothing better for a young girl than an
old horse."

Cowboy Tony gently tugged on the green tops of the carrot, sliding it easily out of the tilled soil. He gave the root a shake that sent small clumps of dirt flying. Reaching down for his pile of carrots he heard, "Caught you orange-handed, you scoundrel!"

Grandma Idaho held Edie by the hand and walked up to the thief with a big smile on her face.
"Just the cowboy I was looking for. These for Hazel?" she asked pointing to the carrots.

"Yep," answered Cowboy Tony. "Ran out this mornin' and you know she doesn't look forward to anything more than a sweet carrot and . . . ."

Cowboy Tony's words trailed off around the bend as he took notice of what was hanging on to the end of Grandma Idaho's hand.

"Howdy there, lil Miss. What's your name?" asked Cowboy Tony in his most polite manner.

The very next morning as the sun peeked over the top of Red Devil Mountain, Cowboy Tony had a little talk with Hazel.

"Now, Ol' Girl," he said as he cleaned and filed her hooves. "I know you've been growing a bit tired of only me for company. You've probably heard my stories a thousand times and I greatly appreciate you being lady enough to put up with them. Needless to say, I feel it may be time for you to make a new friend. Maybe someone you could teach a thing or two."

Hazel listened to Cowboy Tony as she enjoyed her pedicure. She hadn't the slightest what this crazy cowboy was talking about as she loved his daily visits and tall tales more than anything. But, she had to admit she was curious and there was that scent of adventure that wouldn't let her be.

In fact, it was just getting stronger.

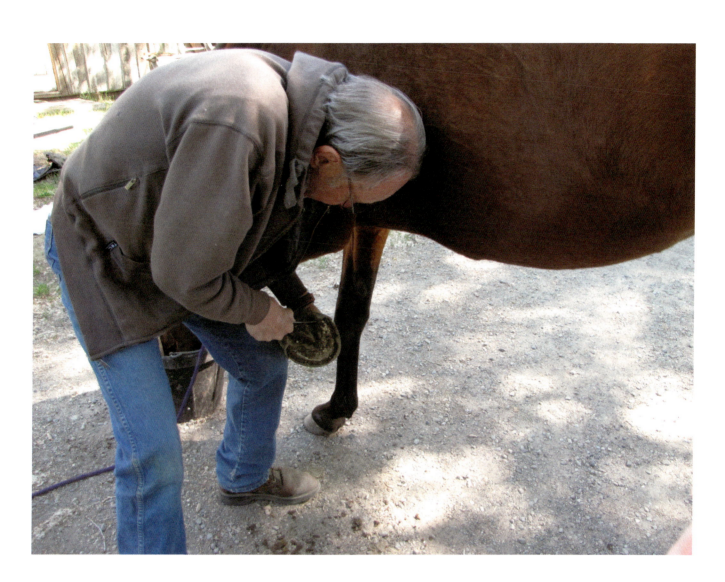

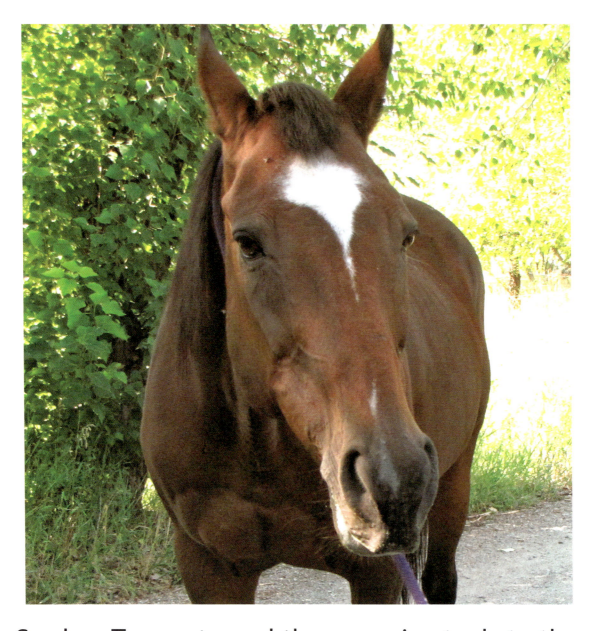

As Cowboy Tony returned the grooming tools to the shed, the sound of a truck rolling over gravel scattered Hazel's thoughts.

The vehicle came to a stop near the pasture gate and a short human opened the door and climbed out.

Hazel stared at the small figure standing shyly before her and sniffed the breeze that surrounded this stranger. The air smelled of cedar trees and roses and rain.

"She must be a jockey," Hazel thought to herself. "She's certainly small enough."

Hazel felt a little sorry for the timid jockey, but mostly wondered, "How the heck am I going to win any races with this mouse at the reins?"

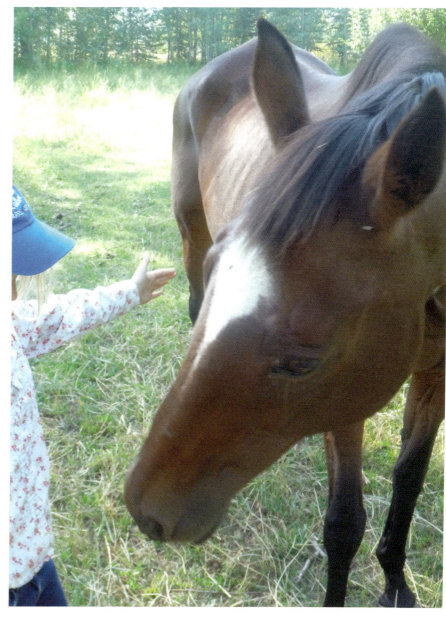

Edie gazed into the big brown eyes
of the horse named Hazel and saw a gentle beast
looking back at her.

Edie's grasshopper feet hopped around
inside her boots and her happy thumbs let loose
of her belt loops to reach up and touch Hazel's
beautiful, soft face.

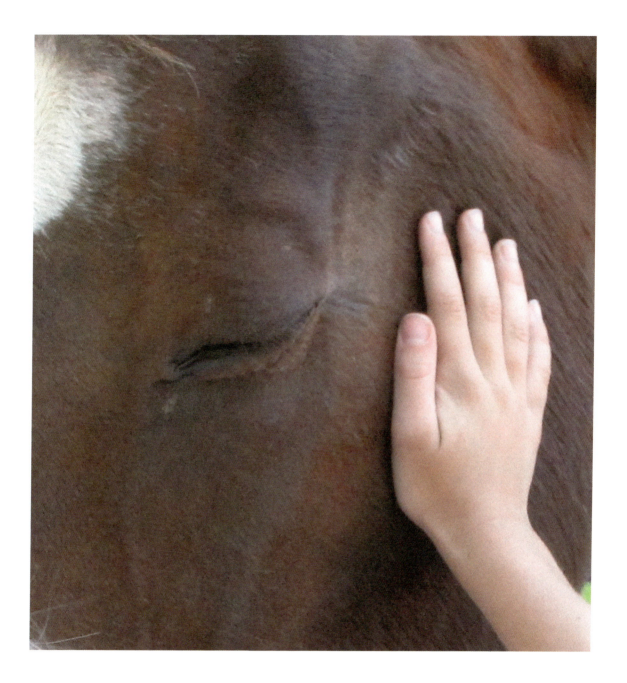

"What a strange and wonderful jockey,"
thought Hazel.

Every morning Edie harvested tasty treats for Hazel from Grandma Idaho's garden.

Her cowgirl clothes literally jumped onto her body in excitement of meeting Cowboy Tony at the pasture where Hazel was always waiting.

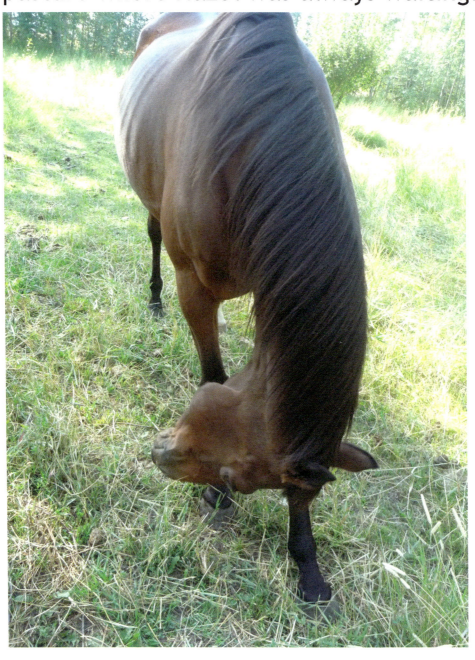

Hazel grew to love the timid jockey who at first squirmed upon her back and couldn't last more than five minutes at a time.

Hazel found she thought less about race tracks and gold cups and more about her little friend who was growing more confident every day.

Cowboy Tony watched as the girls got to know each other.

He smiled seeing Hazel remember her thoroughbred self.

She wasn't just Hazel with Edie, she was Hazel the Wonderhorse.

And, on the back of Hazel, Edie was the world's best jockey.

Cowboy Tony chuckled to himself,

"There is simply nothing better for an old horse than a young girl.

And, there is simply nothing better for a young girl than an old horse."

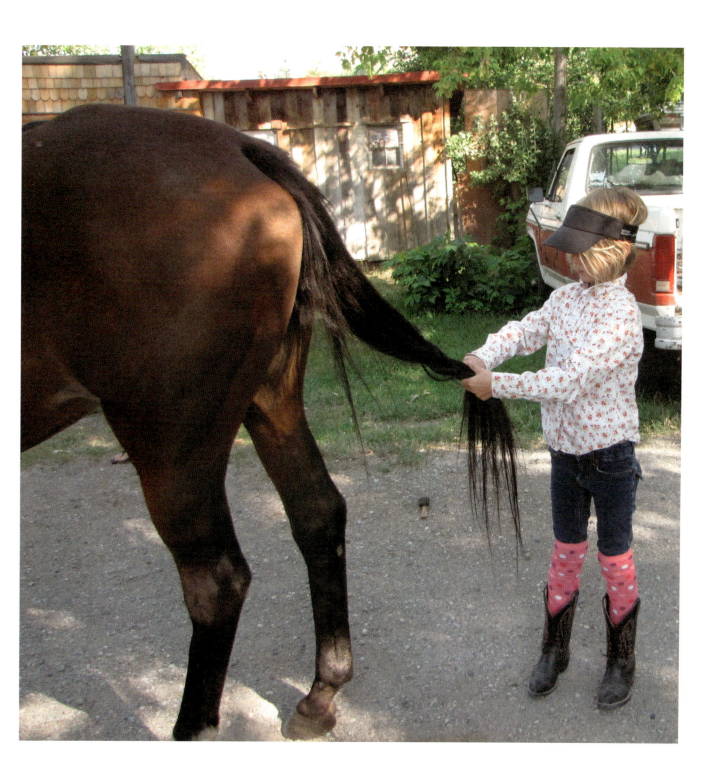

Their tale continues, but sadly
this is the end of the book.

Thank you to the stars of this story:

Grandma & Grandpa Smith
Tony Taylor
Edie Padulo
&
Hazel the Wonderhorse

Made in the USA
Charleston, SC
18 February 2013